اللَّهُمَّ بَلِّغْنا رَمَضان

O Allah, Let Us Reach

Ramadan

**Essential Prayers
& Supplications
for Ramadan
& Eid Ul-Fitr**

Mourad Diouri

مراد الديوري

1

First published in 2024

By Mosaic Tree Press

ISBN 978-1-916524-54-5

Copyright © 2024 Mourad Diouri

Book Design & Typesetting: Mosaic Tree Press

Browse our complete catalogue of publications at
MosaicTree.org

Published by
Mosaic Tree Press

بسم الله الرحمن الرحيم

In the name of God, the Most Gracious, the Most Merciful

اللَّهُمَّ

اللَّهُمَّ
أَهِلَّهُ عَلَيْنا
بِالأَمْنِ وَالإِيمانِ
وَالسَّلامةِ
وَالإِسْلامِ

Allāhumma

Oh Allah

allāhumma 'ahillahu ʿalaynā bil 'amni wal 'īmāni was-salāmati wal-'islami

Allah, bring it over us with blessing and faith, and security and Islam.

When should I say this prayer?

The prayer is read when sighting the new moon, especially at the start of Ramadan, Shawwāl, and Dhul-Hijjah. It seeks Allah's blessings for the new month, asking for security, faith, safety, and guidance in Islam.

الحَمْدُ لِلَّه

الحَمْدُ لِلَّه
الَّذي أَحْيانا
بَعْدَما أَماتَنا
وَإِلَيْهِ النُّشور

Alḥamdulillāh

Praise be to Allah

*alḥamdulillāhi lladhī ʿaḥyānā baʿdamā
ʿamātanā wa ʾilayhin-nushūr*

**All praise is for Allah who gave
us life after having taken it from
us and unto Him is the
resurrection.**

When should I say this prayer?

This prayer is often recited after waking up in
the morning. It's a way to express gratitude to
Allah for the gift of life and to acknowledge
the belief in resurrection on the Day of
Judgment.

بِسْمِ اللّٰه

بِسْمِ اللّٰه

8

Bismillāh

In the name of Allah

bismillāh

In the name of Allah.

When should I say this prayer?

Known as Basmalah (بسملة), it is commonly said before starting any task, action, or activity, seeking Allah's blessings and assistance.

بِسْمِ اللّٰه

بِسْمِ اللّٰهِ
أَوَّلِهِ
وَآخِرِهِ

Bismillāh

In the name of Allah

bismillah 'awwalihi wa 'ākhirihi

In the name of Allah in the beginning and end.

When should I say this prayer?

↳ Often said when forgetting to say Bismillah (before eating or any other action).

الْحَمْدُ لله

الْحَمْدُ لِلَّهِ الَّذِى أَطْعَمَنَا وَسَقَانَا وَجَعَلنَا مُسْلِمِين

Alḥamdulillāh

Praise be to Allah

alḥamdulillāhil-ladhī aṭʿamanā, wa saqānā, wajʿalnā muslimīn

All praise belongs to Allah, who fed us, quenched our thirst, and made us Muslims.

When should I say this prayer?

This prayer of gratitude is often said after finishing a meal or upon receiving sustenance, acknowledging Allah's provisions and their status as Muslims.

الله

وَبِصَوْمِ
غَدٍ نَوَيْتُ
مِنْ شَهْرِ رَمَضَانَ

Allāh
Oh Allah

wa biṣawmi ghaḋinn nawaiytu min ɗhahri ramaḋān

I intend to keep the fast for tomorrow in the month of Ramadan.

When should I say this prayer?

When intending to begin your fast of the first day of Ramadan. It signifies the intention to observe fasting from dawn until sunset the next day, as an act of worship and obedience to Allah's commandments during the holy month of Ramadan.

بِسْمِ اللّٰه

بِسْمِ اللّٰه
وَعَلَى بَرَكَةِ
اللّٰه

Bismillāh

In the name of Allah

bismillāh waʿalā barakattil-lāh

In the name of Allah and with the blessings of Allah I begin (eating).

When should I say this prayer?

This prayer is commonly said before starting any activity, invoking Allah's name and seeking His blessings for success and protection throughout the endeavour.

الْحَمْدُ لِلّه

الْحَمْدُ لِلّه
الَّذي أَطْعَمَني هذا
وَرَزَقَنيهِ
مِنْ غَيْرِ
حَوْلٍ مِنّي
وَلا قُوَّة

Alhamdulillāh

Praise be to Allah

alḥamdu lillāhil-ladhī aṭʿamanī hādha warazaqanīhi min ghayri ḥawlin minnī walā quwwah

All praise is for Allah who fed me this and provided it for me without any might nor power from myself.

When should I say this prayer?

This is a longer version of Alhamdulillāh. It's often recited after receiving a meal or any provision, acknowledging Allah's grace and recognising one's dependency on Him for sustenance.

أَعوذُ بِاللّٰهِ

أَعوذُ بِاللّٰه مِنَ الشَّيْطان الرَّجيم

aʿūdhu billāhi minash-shaytānir-rajīm

I seek refuge with Allah from the cursed Satan.

When should I say this prayer?

Often recited before reciting the Quran, seeking protection from the whispers and temptations of Satan.

صَدَقَ اللهُ الْعَظِيمْ

صَدَقَ اللهُ الْعَظيم

ṣadaqa-llāhu l-aẓīm

Allah has spoken the truth.

When should I say this prayer?

Often said after finishing reciting the Quran
or when affirming the truthfulness of a
statement attributed to Allah or His
Messenger, Muhammad ﷺ (peace be upon
him).

الْحَمْدُ لِلَّه

الْحَمْدُ لِلَّه

al-ḥamdulillāh

All praise is due to God (Tahmid تَحْمِيد) (33 times)

When should I say this prayer?

Alhamdulillah is s an expression of gratitude and acknowledgment of Allah's blessings. It is frequently recited by Muslims in various situations to show appreciation for the countless favours and provisions they receive from Allah.

اللّٰهُ أَكْبَرُ

allāhu 'akbar

God is Greater [than everything] (Takbeer تَكْبِير) (33 times)

When should I say this prayer?

Allahu Akbar is one of the most commonly recited phrases in Islam, often said in various contexts such as during prayer, when praising Allah's greatness, or when expressing awe and gratitude.

سُبْحَانَ اللَّه

سُبْحانَ اللَّه

subḥānallāh

Glorified is God (Tasbih تَسْبِيح)
(33 times)

When should I say this prayer?

↳ Often recited as a form of praise and acknowledgment of Allah's perfection and transcendence. It's used to express reverence and awe towards Allah, the Creator.

لَا إِلَهَ إِلَّا الله

lā 'ilāha 'illā llāh

There is none worthy of worship except Allah (Tahlil تَهْلِيل)(33 times)

When should I say this prayer?

Reciting the declaration of faith (Shahāda) is a way to affirm the oneness of Allah and the rejection of any partners or gods besides Him.

أَسْتَغْفِرُ الله

أَسْتَغْفِرُ الله

'astaghfirullāh

I seek forgiveness from Allah, May Allah forgive me.

When should I say this prayer?

This short prayer is commonly recited as an acknowledgment of our sins and a request for Allah's mercy and forgiveness. Asking for forgiveness is an important aspect of Islamic faith and practice.

سُبْحَانَ اللّٰه.

سُبْحَانَهُ وَتَعَالى

ṣubḥānahu wa taʿālā

Highly praised and glorified is He (Allah)

When should I say this prayer?

This phrase is commonly used after mentioning the name of Allah to glorify and exalt Him. It's often used in various contexts, such as in prayers, recitations of the Quran, or when describing Allah's attributes in discussions or sermons.

عَزَّ وَجَلَّ

عَزَّ وَجَلَّ

ʿazza wa jalla

Mighty and Majestic is He (Allah)

When should I say this prayer?

Often said when referring to Allah in a respectful and reverent manner, particularly when mentioning His attributes of might, glory, and greatness.

جَلَّ جَلَالَه

jalla jalāluhu

Glorified and exalted is He (Allah)

When should I say this prayer?

This phrase is read upon hearing the name of Allah mentioned as a form of reverence used to glorify and magnify His name.

صَلَّى الله عَلَيْهِ وَسَلَّم

ṣallā-llāhu ʿalayhi wa sallam

May the peace and blessings of Allah be upon him.

When should I say this prayer?

Frequently recited after mentioning the name of the Prophet Muhammad ﷺ (peace be upon him) as a sign of respect and reverence.

اللَّهُمَّ

اللَّهُمَّ
أَعِنِّي عَلَى
ذِكْرِكَ وَشُكْرِكَ
وَحُسْنِ عِبادَتِك

Allāhumma
Oh Allah

'allāhuma 'a'innī 'alā dhikrika washukrika wahusni 'ibādatik

O Allah, help me to remember You, to thank You, and to worship You in the best of manners.

When should I say this prayer?

This prayer is for asking Allah for assistance in maintaining a strong connection with Him through remembrance, gratitude, and worship.

اللَّهُمَّ

اللَّهُمَّ إِنِّي أَسْأَلُكَ الْهُدَى وَالتُّقَى وَالْعَفَافَ وَالْغِنَى

Allāhumma

Oh Allah

allāhumma 'innī 'as'alukal-hudā wat-tuqā wal-'afāfa wal-ghinā

O Allah, I ask You for guidance and piety, abstinence (from the unlawful), modesty, contentment, and sufficiency.

When should I say this prayer?

When seeking guidance, moral uprightness, purity, and contentment from Allah.

حسبي الله

حَسْبِيَ اللهُ
لَا إِلَهَ إِلَّا هُوَ
عَلَيْهِ تَوَكَّلْتُ
وَهُوَ رَبُّ
الْعَرْشِ الْعَظِيمِ

ḥasbiya llāhu lā 'ilāha 'illā huwa 'alayhi
tawakkaltu wa huwa rabbul 'arshil 'aẓīm

Allah is sufficient for me. Lā ilāha illa Huwa (none has the right to be worshipped but He), in Him I put my trust and He is the Lord of the Mighty Throne.

When should I say this prayer?

⤷ Said when seeking reliance on Allah, and recognition of His sovereignty and greatness.

اللَّهُمَّ

اللَّهُمَّ
اهْدِني
وسَدِّدْني

Allāhumma

Oh Allah

allāhummah-dinī wa sadd-didnī

O Allah! Direct me to the Right Path and make me adhere to the Straight Path.

When should I say this prayer?

Said when wishing to ask Allah for direction and guidance.

اللَّهُمَّ

اللَّهُمَّ انْفَعْني بِمَا عَلَّمْتَني وَعَلِّمْني مَا يَنْفَعُني وَزِدْني عِلْمًا

Allāhumma

Oh Allah

allāhumma-nfaʿnī bimā ʿallamtanī wa ʿallimnī mā yanfaʿunī wa ziðnī ʿilmā

O Allah, benefit me with what You have taught me, and teach me that which will benefit me, and increase me in knowledge.

When should I say this prayer?

⤷ When seeking Allah's assistance in gaining beneficial knowledge and wisdom.

اللَّهُمَّ

اللَّهُمَّ عافِنِي فِي بَدَنِي
اللَّهُمَّ عافِنِي فِي سَمْعِي
اللَّهُمَّ عافِنِي فِي بَصَرِي
لا إِلٰهَ إِلاَّ أَنْتَ
اللَّهُمَّ إِنِّي أَعُوذُ بِكَ
مِنَ الْكُفْرِ وَالْفَقْرِ
وَأَعُوذُ بِكَ مِنْ عَذابِ الْقَبْرِ
لا إِلٰهَ إِلاَّ أَنْتَ

Allāhumma
Oh Allah

allāhumma 'āfinī fī badanī, Allāhumma 'āfinī fī sam'ī, allāhumma 'āfinī fī baṣarī, lā 'ilāha 'illā 'anta. allāhumma 'innī 'a'ūdhu bika minal-kufri, walfaqri, wa 'a'ūdhu bika min 'adhābil-qabri, lā 'ilāha 'illā 'anta

O Allah, make me healthy in my body. O Allah, preserve for me my hearing. O Allah, preserve for me my sight. There is none worthy of worship but You . O Allah , I seek refuge in You from disbelief and poverty and I seek refuge in You from the punishment of the grave. There is none worthy of worship but You.

When should I say this prayer?

This comprehensive prayer is a way of asking for physical well-being, protection from spiritual ailments, and seeking refuge in Allah from worldly and hereafter afflictions.

اللَّهُمَّ

لَا حَوْلَ وَلَا قُوَّةَ إِلَّا بِاللهِ

Allāhumma

Oh Allah

la ḥawla walā quwwata 'illā billāh

There is no power nor strength except that gained through Allah.

When should I say this prayer?

This prayer - known as Hawqalah (حوقلة) is often recited during times of difficulty or when facing challenges, reminding themselves and others of their dependence on Allah's help and strength.

رَبّ

Rabbi

رَبِّ
ارْحَمْهُما
كَما رَبَّياني صَغيرًا

Allāhumma

Oh Allah

rabbi-rḥamhumā kamā rabbayāni ṣaghīra

My Lord, have mercy upon them (parents) as they brought me up [When I was] small.

When should I say this prayer?

This prayer is lovingly said when seeking Allah's mercy for our parents, showing appreciation for their nurturing and upbringing.

اللَّهُمَّ

اللَّهُمَّ لا سَهْلَ
إِلاَّ مَا جَعَلْتَهُ
سَهْلاً وَأَنْتَ تَجْعَلُ
الْحَزَنَ إِذَا شِئْتَ
سَهْلاً

Allāhumma
Oh Allah

*allāhuma la sahla ʾillā mā jaʿaltahu sahlan
wa ʾanta tajʿalul-ḥazna ʾiḏhā shiʾta sahlan*

O Allah, there is no ease except in that which You have made easy, and You make the difficulty, if You wish, easy.

When should I say this prayer?

This prayer is typically said when facing challenges or difficulties, affirming that there is no ease except what Allah makes easy, and that Allah can make hardship easy if He wills.

اللَّهُمَّ

اللَّهُمَّ

لَكَ صُمْتُ

وَبِكَ آمَنْتُ

وَعَلَيْكَ تَوَكَّلْتُ

وَعَلَى رِزْقِكَ أَفْطَرْتُ

Allāhumma
Oh Allah

allahumma laka ṣumtu, wa bika āmantu, wa 'layka tawakkaltu, wa 'la rizqika afṭartu

Oh Allah! I fasted for You and I believe in You [and I put my trust in You] and I break my fast with Your sustenance.

When should I say this prayer?

This prayer is said **when opening or breaking your fast** before you begin Iftar (إفــطار) (the meal that breaks the fast) at sunset. It's a prayer to express gratitude for relief from thirst and hope for future blessings.

بِاللَّه

ذَهَبَ الظَّمَأُ
وابْتَلَّتِ العُروقُ
وَثَبَتَ الأَجْرُ
إِنْ شاءَ الله
تَعالى

Allāh
Oh Allah

ḏhahabaẓ-ẓamaʿu wabtallatil- ʿurūq wa thabatal- ʿajru ʿinshāʾllāh taʿālā

The thirst is gone, the veins are moistened, and the reward has been earned if Allah wills.

When should I say this prayer?

This prayer is said **when opening or breaking your fast** before you begin Iftar (إفطار) (the meal that breaks the fast) at sunset. It's a prayer to express gratitude for relief from thirst and hope for future blessings.

اللَّهُمَّ

أَفْطَرَ
عِنْدَكُمُ الصَّائِمونَ
وَأَكَلَ طعَامَكُمُ الأبرارُ
وَصَلَّت عَلَيْكُمُ
الملائِكةُ
وَذَكَرَكُم اللهُ
فيمَن عِنْدَهُ

Allāhumma

Oh Allah

'afṭara 'indakumṣ-ṣā'imūn wa 'akala ṭa'āmakum al-abrār, wa ṣallat 'alaikuml-malā 'ika wa ḏhakrakum-llāh fīman 'indahu

May the fasting people break fast at your place, may the pious eat from your food, and may the angels pray for you.

When should I say this prayer?

Often read when breaking our fast with friends, family and loved ones, particularly when graciously invited by others.

رَبّ

Rabbi

رَبِّ

اغْفِرْ لِي ذُنُوبِي

وَافْتَحْ لِي أَبْوابَ رَحْمَتِكَ

Rabbi
Oh Allah

rabbighfir lī ∂hunūbī waiftah lī ʿabwāba rahmatika

O Lord, forgive my sins and open the doors of mercy for me.

When should I say this prayer?

Commonly said when **entering** the mosque. It's a plea for Allah's forgiveness and blessings.

رَبّ

Rabbi

رَبِّ
اغْفِرْ لي ذُنوبِي
وَافْتَحْ لي أَبْوابَ فَضْلِكَ

Rabbi
Oh Allah

rabbi ghfir lī ðhunūbī wa-ftaḥ lī 'abwāba faðlika

O Lord, pardon my sins and open the doors of virtue for me.

When should I say this prayer?

Commonly said when **leaving** the mosque. It's a plea for Allah's forgiveness and blessings.

اللَّهُمَّ

اللَّهُمَّ
رَبَّ هَذِهِ الدَّعْوَةِ التَّامَّةِ
وَالصَّلَاةِ الْقَائِمَةِ
آتِ مُحَمَّداً الْوَسِيلَةَ
وَالْفَضِيلَةَ
وَابْعَثْهُ مَقَاماً مَحْمُوداً
الَّذِي وَعَدْتَهُ إِنَّكَ
لَا تُخْلِفُ الْمِيعَاد

Allāhumma

Oh Allah

allāhumma rabba hādhih-da'wati t-tāmma waṣ-ṣalātil-qā'ima, 'āti Muhammadan il-wasīla walfaḍhīla, wab 'at-hu maqāmam mahmūdanil-ladhī wa 'adtahu, 'innaka lā tukhliful-mī'ād

O Allah, Lord of this perfect call and established prayer Grant Muhammad the intercession and favor, and raise him to the honored station You have promised him, [verily You do not neglect promises.

When should I say this prayer?

Often recited after hearing the Adhān (call to prayer) and before the Iqāma (second call to prayer) in congregational prayers.

اللَّهُمَّ

بِاسْمِكَ
اللَّهُمَّ
أَمُوت وأَحْيا

Allāhumma
Oh Allah

bismika-llāhumma ʿamūtu wa ʿaḥyā

In Your name O Allah, I live and die.

When should I say this prayer?

This prayer is said before going to sleep and it is a recognition of Allah's control over life and death as you prepare to rest.

اللَّهُمَّ

اللَّهُمَّ
إِنَّكَ عَفُوٌّ كَرِيمٌ
تُحِبُّ الْعَفْوَ
فَاعْفُ عَنِّي

Allāhumma

Oh Allah

allāhumma ʿinnaka ʿafuwwun karīm tuḥibbul-ʿafwa faʿfu ʿannī

O Allah, indīd You are Pardoning, [Generous,] You love pardon, so pardon me.

When should I say this prayer?

This prayer is a humble request for Allah's forgiveness, acknowledging His merciful nature and His love for pardoning His servants. This prayer stands among the most frequently suggested prayers for Laylat Al-Qadr (The Night of Power ليلة القدر) in the last 10 days of Ramadan.

اللَّهُمَّ

اللَّهُمَّ أَجِرْني مِنَ النَّارِ

Allāhumma
Oh Allah

allāhumma 'ajirnī minan-nār

O Allah, I seek your protection from the hellfire.

When should I say this prayer?

⤷ This prayer is recommended to recite during the last 10 days of Ramadan seeking refuge from the hellfire.

اللَّهُمَّ

اللَّهُمَّ
إِنِّي أَسْأَلُكَ
رِضَاكَ وَالْجَنَّةَ
وَأَعُوذُ بِكَ
مِنْ سَخَطِكَ وَالنَّارِ

Allāhumma

Oh Allah

allāhumma ʿinnī ʿas-ʿaluka riḍāka wal-jannah wa ʿaʿuḍhu bika min sakhaṭika wan-nār

O Allah, I ask of Your pleasure and for Paradise, and I seek refuge from Your displeasure and from the Hellfire.

When should I say this prayer?

This prayer is for seeking Allah's pleasure and Paradise while seeking protection from His anger and the punishment of Hellfire.

اللّٰهُمَّ

يَا حَيُّ

يَا قَيُّومُ

بِرَحْمَتِكَ

أَسْتَغِيثُ

Allāhumma
Oh Allah

ya ḥayyu yā qayyum bi raḥmatika astaghīth

Oh Everliving, The Everlasting, I seek Your help through Your mercy.

When should I say this prayer?

This prayer is a plea for assistance and support, calling upon Allah's attributes of eternal life and sustenance, and seeking refuge in His mercy.

اللَّهُمَّ

أَسْتَغْفِرُ
اللهَ رَبِّي
مِنْ كُلِّ ذَنْبٍ
وَأَتوبُ إِلَيْه

Allāhumma

Oh Allah

astagfirullāha rabbī min kulli dhanbin wa-ʿatūbu ʿilaiyh

I seek forgiveness from Allah for all my sins and turn to Him.

When should I say this prayer?

This supplication is a plea for forgiveness from Allah. It's a heartfelt request for Allah's forgiveness, acknowledging our shortcomings and seeking His mercy.

اللَّهُمَّ

اللَّهُمَّ
إِنِّي ظَلَمْتُ نَفْسِي
ظُلْمًا كَثِيرًا
وَلَا يَغْفِرُ الذُّنوبَ
إِلَّا أَنْتَ فَاغْفِرْ لِي
مَغْفِرَةً مِنْ عِنْدِكَ
وَارْحَمْنِي إِنَّكَ أَنْتَ
الغَفورُ الرَّحِيمُ

Allāhumma
Oh Allah

allahumma 'innī ẓalamtu nafsī ẓulman kathīran walā yaghfiru-ddhunūba 'illā anta faghfir lī maghfiratam-min 'indika warḥamnī 'innaka anta-l-ghafūru-rraḥīm

O Allah! I have greatly wronged myself and none forgives sins except You, so grant me Your forgiveness and have mercy on me. You are the Forgiving, the Merciful.

When should I say this prayer?

This supplication is a plea for forgiveness from Allah. It's a heartfelt request for Allah's forgiveness, acknowledging our shortcomings and seeking His mercy.

اللَّهُمَّ

اللّهُمَّ
إِنِّي عَبْدُكَ
ابْنُ عَبْدِكَ
ابْنُ أَمَتِكَ ناصِيَتِي بِيَدِكَ
ماضٍ فيَّ حُكْمُكَ
عَدْلٌ فيَّ قَضاؤُكَ
أَسْأَلُكَ بِكُلِّ اسْمٍ هُوَ لَكَ
سَمَّيْتَ بِهِ نَفْسَكَ
أَوْ أَنْزَلْتَهُ في كِتابِكَ
أَوْ عَلَّمْتَهُ أَحَداً مِنْ خَلْقِكَ
أَوِ اسْتَأْثَرْتَ بِهِ في عِلْمِ الغَيْبِ عِنْدَكَ
أَنْ تَجْعَلَ القُرْآنَ رَبِيعَ قَلْبِي
وَنورَ صَدْرِي وجَلاءَ حُزْنِي
وذَهابَ هَمّي

Allāhumma

Oh Allah

*allāhumma 'innī 'abduka, ibnu 'abdika, ibnu 'amatik, nāṣiyatī
biyadik, mādin fiyya ḥukmuk, 'adlun fiyya qaḍā'uk, as'aluka bikulli
ismin huwa lak, sammayta bihi nafsak, 'aw 'anzaltahu fī kitābik, 'aw
'allamtahu aḥadan min khalqik 'aw is-ta'tharta bihi fī 'ilmil-ghaybi
'indak, 'an taj'alal Qur'āna rabī'a qalbī, wanūra ṣadrī, wajalā'
ḥuznī wa-dhaahaba hammī*

O Allah, I am Your servant, son of Your servant,
son of Your maidservant, my forelock is in Your
hand (ie You have total mastery over), Your
command over me is forever executed and Your
decree over me is just I ask You by every name
belonging to You which You named Yourself with,
or revealed in Your Book, or You taught to any of
Your creation, or You have preserved in the
knowledge of the unseen with You, that You make
the Quran the life of my heart and the light of my
breast, and a departure for my sorrow and a release
for my anxiety

When should I say this prayer?

Known as the Du'ā' Al-Qunūt, it is a prayer
to ask for guidance, mercy, and support from
Allah, using various beautiful names and
attributes of Allah and seeking His help in
various matters of life.

اللَّهُمَّ

لَا إِلَهَ إِلَّا اللهُ الْعَظِيمُ الْحَلِيمْ

لَا إِلَهَ إِلَّا اللهُ

رَبُّ الْعَرْشِ الْعَظِيمِ

لَا إِلَهَ إِلَّا اللهُ

رَبُّ السَّمواتِ

ورَبُّ الأَرْضِ

ورَبُّ الْعَرْشِ الكَرِيم

Allāhumma
Oh Allah

lā 'ilāha 'illāl-lāhul ʿaẓīmul-ḥalīm, lā 'ilāha 'illāl-lāhu rabbul-ʿarshil ʿaẓīm, lā 'ilāha 'illāl-lāhu rabbus-samāwāti warabbul ʿarḍi warabbul ʿarshil-karīm

None has the right to be worshipped except Allah Forbearing None has the right to be worshipped except Allah, Lord of the magnificent throne None has the right to be worshipped except Allah, Lord of the heavens, Lord of the Earth and Lord of the noble throne.

When should I say this prayer?

Often recited in situations where you seek comfort, strength, or solace. It's a declaration of faith in the greatness, patience, and sovereignty of Allah. You may recite it during times of difficulty, distress, or when feeling overwhelmed, as a way to remind yourself of the power and mercy of Allah.

الْحَمْدُ لِله

الْحَمْدُ لله
الَّذِي كَسَانِي
هَذَا وَرَزَقَنِيهِ
مِنْ غَيْرِ حَوْلٍ
مِنِّي وَلَا قُوَّةٍ

Alhamdulillāh

Praise be to Allah

*alhamdu lillāhil-ladhī kasānī hāthā wa razaqanīhi
min ghayri ḥawlim-minnī wa-lā quwwatin*

**Praise is to Allah Who has clothed me
with this (garment) and provided it
for me, though I was powerless myself
and incapable.**

When should I say this prayer?

Often recited when wearing new clothes for
Eid (or any other occasion), praising Allah
for providing the garment and
acknowledging one's reliance solely on Him.

اللَّهُمَّ

اللَّهُمَّ
اجْعَلْهَا مَغْنَمًا
وَلاَ تَجْعَلْهَا مَغْرَمًا

Allāhumma

Oh Allah

*allahummaj-'alha maghnaman wa la taj-
'alha maghrama*

O Allah, make it a gain and do not make it a loss.

When should I say this prayer?

⌐⟶ Said when wishing to pay "Zakat-ul-
Fitr" (Charity of breaking the fast of
Ramadan)

اللَّه

اللهُ أَكْبَرُ

اللهُ أَكْبَرُ

لَا إِلَهَ إِلَّا الله

وَاَللهُ أَكْبَرُ

اللهُ أَكْبَرُ

وَلِلَّهِ الْحَمْدُ

Allāh

Oh Allah

allāhu akbar, allāhu akbar, lā 'ilāha illallāh,
wallāhu akbar, allāhu akbar wa lillāhil ḥamd

Allah is the greatest, Allah is the greatest, there is no god but Allah. And Allah is the greatest, Allah is the greatest and to Allah belongs all praise.

When should I say this prayer?

This prayer is known as Takbirāt Al-ʿeid (تكبيرات العيد), often recited during while walking to the mosque on Eid day and during Eid prayers as well as other joyous occasions in Islam. It's a proclamation of the greatness of Allah and a declaration of His absolute sovereignty and praise.

عيد سَعيد

عيد مُبارَك
عيد سَعيد
كُلُّ عامٍ وَ أَنْتُم بِخَيْر

ʿīd mubārak / ʿīd ṣa ʿīd /   Kullu ʿāmin wa ʾantum bikhair

Blessed Eid (feast/festival)

Happy Eid

May you be well with every passing year

When should I say this prayer?

Usually said when greeting and congratulating your family & friends on Eid day

عيد سعيد

تَقَبَّلَ اللهُ مِنّا وَمِنْكُم

taqabbala-llāhu minnā wa minkum

May Allah accept from you and us

When should I say this prayer?

↳ Usually said when greeting and
congratulating your family & friends
on Eid day

About the Author

Mourad Diouri is an author and teaching fellow of Arabic at the University of Edinburgh in Scotland, UK. In addition to writing instructional books on learning Arabic as a foreign language, he also works as an education consultant, external examiner and teacher trainer within the UK and internationally. He lives in Edinburgh, Scotland, with his wife and children.

Also by Mourad Diouri

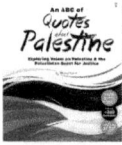

An ABC of Quotes About Palestine: Exploring Voices on Palestine & the Palestinian Quest for Justice (2023)

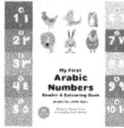

My First Arabic Numbers Reader & Colouring Book, (2023)

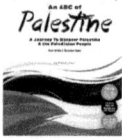

An Abc of Palestine: A Journey To Discover Palestine & The Palestinian People For Kids & Grown Ups (2023)

My First Arabic Colours: Reader & Activity Book for Kids, (2023)

My Journey Through The Most Beautiful Names of Allah: Arabic Reader & Activity Book for Kids: **(Volume 1, 2 & 3)** (2023)

My Arabic Learning Journals: My Abc Dictionary (English-Arabic), (2022)

My First Arabic Alphabet & Colouring Book [Arabic for Little Ones] (2023)

My Arabic Learning Journals: My Abc Dictionary (Arabic- English), (2022)

My Arabic Animal Alphabet Reader, Arabic for Little Ones, (2023)

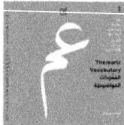

My Arabic Learning Journals: Thematic Vocabulary, (2022)

My First Arabic Alphabet Reader, Arabic for Little Ones, (2023)

Tricky Tongue Twisters In Arabic (Arabic Script & Sounds), [Essential Arabic Readers] (2023)

My Journey through Ramadan & Eid Al-Fitr (Arabic for Little Ones), Mosaic Tree Press (2023)

CoronaVirus Lexicon: A Practical Guide for Arabic Learners & Translators (M. Diouri & M. Aboelezz 2023)

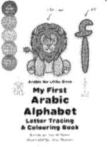

My First Arabic Alphabet: Letter Tracing & Colouring Book [Arabic for Little Ones] (2023)

Listen, Read & Write: Arabic Alphabet Letter Groups [Essential Arabic Readers] (2023)

Essential Arabic Readers: Arabic Alphabet Writing Practice Handbook, Mosaic Tree Press (2023)

Essential Arabic Readers: Alphabet Letters with Vowels & Pronunciation Symbols, Mosaic Tree Press (2022)

Arabic & Islamic Mosaic & Calligraphy Colouring Journal (Volume 1: Islamic Quotes) (2022)

Arabic Alphabet: 25+ Cut-Out Displays for Self-Study & Classroom Use (Visual & Playful Arabic) (2023)

I Am .... An ABC of Empowering Self-Affirmations: A Guided Journal for Self-Discovery, Self-Growth & Resilience

My Lord (ربّ): Qur'anic Prayers for Daily Blessings & Inspiration (O Lord 365) (2024)

O Allah, Let Us Reach Ramadan (اللهم بلغنا رمضان): Essential Prayers & Supplications for Ramadan & Eid Ul-Fitr (O Lord 365) (2024)

Our Lord (ربّـنـا): Qur'anic Prayers for Daily Blessings & Inspiration (O Lord 365) (2024)

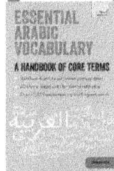

Teach Yourself: Essential Arabic Vocabulary: A Handbook of Core Terms, Hodder Education (2015)

Internet Arabic: Essential Middle Eastern Vocabularies (w/ MP3 CD), Edinburgh University Press (2013)

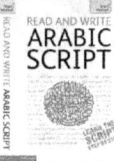

Teach Yourself: Read & Write Arabic Script, Hodder Education (2011)

Browse our full catalogue at

MosaicTree.org

Arabic Script &
Sounds

Arabic Vocabulary

Arabic for Little
Ones

Arabic/Islamic Mosaic
& Calligraphy

Arabic Learning
Journals

Well-Being & Character
Development

Mosaic Tree Press
MosaicTree.org

Completed with the grace of God